Hawkins 1992

# The Mother Teresa Story

*By Maria Shrady*
*Illustrated by Frederick Shrady*

PAULIST PRESS
New York/Mahwah

Book design by Celine M. Allen.

Cover illustration by Marina Shrady.

Copyright © 1987 by
Maria Shrady

All rights reserved. No part of this book may be reproduced or transmitted in
any form or by any means, electronic or mechanical, including photocopying,
recording or by any information storage and retrieval system without permission in writing from the publisher.

Library of Congress Cataloging-in-Publication Data

Shrady, Maria.
     The Mother Teresa story.

     Summary: Describes the life of the European nun who
went to India as a missionary, followed the call of God
to found a new order, and gained wide recognition and the
Nobel Peace Prize for her work with the sick and the
destitute.
     1. Teresa, Mother, 1910-      —Juvenile literature.
2. Missionaries of Charity—Biography—Juvenile literature,
[1. Teresa, Mother, 1910-         .     2. Nuns.     3. Missionaries.  4. Missionaries of Charity]   I. Shrady, Frederick,
ill.   II. Title.
BX4406.5.Z8C57   1987      271'.97 [B] [92] 87-6871
ISBN 0-8091-6567-8 (pbk.)

Published by Paulist Press
997 Macarthur Boulevard
Mahwah, New Jersey 07430

Printed and bound in the
United States of America

*For Donata and Titina,*
*Alix and Bettina,*
*Benedicta and Verena,*
*Miley and Alexander,*
*Christopher, Peter, and Sophia*

# I

This is the story about a woman many in India and elsewhere in the world simply call "Mother." She was born on August 17, 1910. Her name was Agnes Gonxha Bojaxhiu—this is an Albanian name, and I'll bet you can't pronounce it any better than I can. She had a very happy childhood, because all the members of her family loved each other so much. When she grew up she wore leather shoes that curled up in front, like all the other girls, and a bright kerchief on her head. In the marketplace of a Yugoslav town—the town of Skopje, which borders Albania—there were always plenty of people around. Someone played the accordion, and then everybody started to dance. Next to the church—for the church has a very special place in

1

this girl's life as you will soon discover—children played hoops and hopscotch, as children do the world over. A donkey was sure to be found about somewhere, waiting to take a cartload of pots and pans up the hill.

Mother Teresa, or Agnes, as she was then called, went to the public school. She was a tiny girl, full of life and laughter. When she was twelve years old she became a member of a Sodality, which is another name for a club for young people specially devoted to Our Lady. It was there that she first heard stories about India. Some Yugoslav Jesuits had gone to missions in Bengal, India (remember the Bengal tigers?) and their letters were read aloud at the meetings of the club. After that Agnes knew that she wanted to be a missionary in India. As you may know, a missionary is someone sent out by God, usually to distant lands.

# II

With the help of her friends at the Sodality, Agnes wrote to the Irish Sisters of Loreto, who had missions in Bengal, and when she reached the age of eighteen, she was sent to the Abbey in Dublin, Ireland to study English. Perhaps you know already how difficult it is to learn a foreign language. But then you may have heard some Spanish spoken in the streets, and maybe some French by your parents, or you may have seen it printed on a menu. But for Agnes, who had never left her home town, it was extremely hard. In addition to this she had to say many prayers at odd hours, keep her hands folded in a meek fashion, and observe silence a lot. For if God is to speak, we have to be silent. And she wanted to find out very much what He had in mind for her.

Well, in this first instance she was called to a plantation where tea is grown at Darjeeling, a town on the slopes of the Himalayas. You may have seen the name on your mother's tea can—that is, if she likes tea. Here the Loreto Sisters ran a school, and that is where she began her life as a religious, taking the name of Sister Teresa. After a year she was sent south to Calcutta to teach geography at St. Mary's High School.

Now Calcutta was not a bit like Darjeeling. Rather it was a large, teeming city, the second largest in the British Empire, filled with all the characters and beggars and snake-charmers you have ever read about. St. Mary's was a school in which British and Bengali girls were meant to curtsy prettily and speak with nice accents and have proper table manners, in addition to getting a good education. Sister Teresa learned the languages of Bengali and Hindi here, and her English began to develop Indian cadences.

Considering the kind of person she was, tiny and full of life and laughter, it isn't at all surprising that she was very popular with the girls, and in time she became principal of the school. Sometimes she made trips with her students to the Calcutta slums. But what her dreams were and her fears, nobody knew at the time. Perhaps she didn't even know herself.

# III

One day—and this was an extremely important day; it was September 10, 1946—Sister Teresa was traveling on a train to Darjeeling. Trains are terribly crowded in India, not a bit like commuter trains here, where almost everybody can be pretty sure of getting a seat. In India it is not at all uncommon for people to ride outside the train, clusters of people hanging on for dear life.

It was on such a train that Sister Teresa received a call from God. She called it "a call within a call," for she had already been called to be a Sister of Loreto. But this time she received a call to leave her order and found a new one. God was asking her to leave the comfort of her convent and live among the poorest in the vast city. It was an order, she said. "I

knew where I belonged but I didn't know how to get there."

Now if you believe for one moment that all she really wanted to do was leave her school—as you sometimes do—you are wrong. She loved her school. She said that leaving her school was harder than leaving home. And we all know what "home" means: the love of our family, and security and good meals, and clean sheets at night. From now on she would have none of these things.

One day, while looking for a shelter in the large and turbulent city of Calcutta, she found herself surrounded by hordes of peddlers and beggars. A cyclone of trucks and carts and rickshaws—curious vehicles drawn by humans—swirled around her. Herds of buffalo and cows, driven along with sticks, their bells clanging above the traffic noise, were trying to make their way through the streets. She thought her head was going to burst. She walked and walked—and all this in the paralyzing heat that melted the asphalt beneath her feet—until her arms and legs ached. It made her understand—and we call this understanding "compassion"—how much the poor must ache in body and soul for a home, for food and health.

At that moment she longed for the comfort and cool of Loreto, with the table set and the napkins folded and the bells ringing for prayers. But there she made her choice: "My God," she prayed, "out of love for You I desire to follow Your call and do whatever Your holy will may be for me. Give me courage, right now, this very moment." And she went on her way.

# IV

After permission from the Pope arrived to found a new order—and it took a good long while to obtain it—and just a year and a day after India became an independent nation, Sister Teresa left the Convent of Loreto, where she had been so happy, for the streets and slums of Calcutta. To blend more easily with the people she had set out to serve, she chose the traditional Indian sari as her new habit: a white cotton wrap-around with a blue border and a cross worn on the shoulder.

The first person to join Sister Teresa in her work was a nineteen-year-old Bengali girl named Subshahini Das, who had been a student at the Loreto School. This girl, who was even smaller than Sister Teresa, became the first novice and took on her former teacher's baptismal name, becoming Sister Agnes.

A year and a half after Sister Agnes' arrival, the new Congregation of the Missionaries of Charity was founded in Calcutta, and Sister Teresa became Mother Teresa and an Indian citizen. You know already what a missionary is, but think for a while on the meaning of this word "charity." Does it mean charity as we read of it in the papers: a benefit performance, a charity ball, dropping pennies we don't really need into the collection box? No, it means none of these things. What it means is an overflowing love—a love of God so great that it overflows in love of others. For Mother Teresa sees Jesus in every person, but she sees Him particularly in the poor and the sick who are in need of her love. "The love of the poor," she says, "is an adoration of Christ."

Even people like Mother Teresa do not always see their way clearly mapped out for them. Like Abraham, of whom you have read in the Old Testament, they take one step forward in the dark.

Before Mother Teresa took up her mission in the slums of Calcutta she spent three months with the Medical Missionary Sisters, learning how to take care of the sick. Her plans were rather indefinite at first. But "God showed us what He wanted us to do," she said.

One day in June 1952, after her return to Calcutta, she was walking through the slums with Sister Agnes. A monsoon—a fierce wind from the Indian Ocean—was beating down on Calcutta with a fury that seemed to herald the end of the world.

In the midst of this deluge Mother Teresa suddenly stumbled upon something stretched out on the ground. She stopped and discovered an old woman lying in a pool of water. The woman was barely breathing. Mother Teresa scooped her into her arms and ran to the nearest hospital. She found the Emergency Entrance and placed the dying woman on a stretcher. Instantly an attendant intervened. "Take this woman away immediately!" he ordered. "There's nothing we can do for her." Again Mother Teresa took the woman into her arms and set off at a run. She knew of another hospital not too far away. Suddenly she realized that the woman had died. Putting down her burden, she made the Sign of the Cross and prayed beside her in the rain: "In this city even the dogs are treated better than human beings," she sighed and turned away.

The next morning she went to the Town Hall and besieged the officials. One of the Mayor's deputies finally received her. "It's a disgrace that people in this city are forced to die in the streets!" she declared. "Give me a house where they can die in dignity and know that they are wanted." At that time she had nothing but five rupees—which is just about one dollar—and her faith. But faith, as you know, can move mountains, and one week later the government placed at her disposal a former resthouse for Hindu pilgrims, next to the great Kali Temple.

Now you must know that the Temple of Kali, with its dome that looks like a sugar-loaf, was the most frequented shrine in Calcutta. Day and night swarms of people were crowding around its gray walls. There were beggars and idlers and street urchins, seeking to extort some money from the tourists. Penitents, dressed in white cotton, were leading goats to the sacrifice. Merchants with huge baskets sold flower petals as an offering to Kali, the goddess of destruction. At night thousands of Indians thronged and shoved and waited to file past the temple to gain a glimpse of the idol. It was the most crowded square in the city and the atmosphere was turbulent and aggressive.

Around the corner, in Mother Teresa's building, things were different. There was no door in the imposing archway. Anyone could enter at any time. A wooden sign read NIRMAL HRIDAY, which is Bengali and means THE PLACE OF THE PURE IN HEART.

# VI

To this place Mother Teresa and her Sisters—there were now twenty-six of them—brought the sick and the dying. Before they took over the building, it had fallen into shabbiness and was used by local toughs as a gambling den. When she first started ministering to the sick, the toughs and temple loiterers threw rocks. One day a shower of stones rained down on an ambulance bringing patients to the shelter. The Sisters were insulted and threatened. Eventually Mother Teresa dropped on her knees before the ruffians: "Kill me," she cried in Bengali, her arms outstretched in the Sign of the Cross, "and I'll be in heaven all the sooner!"

The rabble withdrew, but neighborhood delegations complained to the authorities. There had been rumors that this foreign nun was converting the dying to Christianity. The Chief of Police decided to make his own inquiries.

When he entered, he found Mother Teresa kneeling at the bedside of a man who had just been picked off the streets with horrible sores, so horrible that he had been turned away by every hospital. Mother Teresa cleansed the wounds, applied dressings, and assured the poor man that he would get better. His suffering was transformed into surprise and then into peace. Mother Teresa's face was radiating an extraordinary serenity, and the Chief of Police found himself strangely moved. "Would you like me to show you around?" she asked. "No, Mother," he excused himself. "That won't be necessary."

As he left the building, the neighborhood's young fanatics were waiting for him on the steps. "I promised that I would expel the foreign woman," he told them. "And I will do so the day that your mothers and sisters come here and do what she is doing."

The battle, however, was not yet over. Troublemakers continued to throw stones. One morning Mother Teresa noticed a gathering outside the Kali Temple. As she approached, she saw a man lying on the ground, apparently drained of all life. A triple braid knotted at the top of his head denoted that

he was a Brahmin, one of the priests from the temple. A Brahmin belongs to the sacred Hindu caste that claims direct descent from the deity Brahma. No one dared to touch him. They knew he was suffering from cholera, a frightening disease. Mother Teresa bent over, took the body of the Brahmin into her arms and carried him to her shelter, which you remember, is THE PLACE OF THE PURE IN HEART. Day and night she nursed him, and eventually he recovered. One day he exclaimed: "All my life I have worshiped Kali, a goddess of stone; but here is the real Kali, a goddess of flesh and blood!" Never again were stones thrown at the little sisters in the white saris.

News of the incident spread throughout the whole city. Every day ambulances and police vans brought the suffering to Mother Teresa. "NIRMAL HRIDAY is the jewel of Calcutta," she was to say one day. It was granted the protection of the city itself. Today, when Mother Teresa makes her Sunday rounds, the rock-throwers of old touch her feet in a gesture of veneration.

# VII

Because of her compassionate concern for the destitute, Mother Teresa soon came to be known as "The Saint of the Gutters." More and more people began to recognize her. One of these was the most important man in Bengal, the chief minister or governor. He was also a physician and people came to his clinic. Among those who would turn up regularly at six o'clock in the morning was Mother Teresa. However, she didn't come for medical advice. She would wait her turn and then ask how to connect a water main in a slum, or how to obtain electricity for her school. By rising early, she had conquered the red tape that can defeat even the best intentions in India.

The governor became one of Mother Teresa's

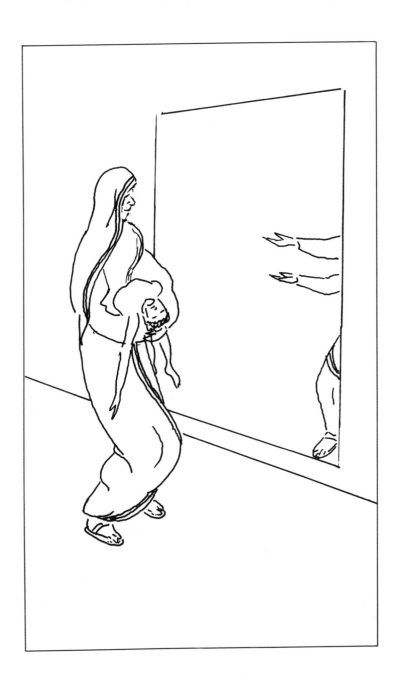

most powerful allies. So did Prime Minister Indira Gandhi, who lent her support to the missionaries. Even young radicals who had turned to terrorism in the 1960's didn't disturb Mother Teresa. "We had no trouble and sometimes they helped us," she said.

Soon volunteers began to arrive from all parts of the world helping to feed the poor. Now you must realize that being poor in India doesn't just mean lacking vitamins in your diet or living in a crowded place. It means making your house on the pavement with not even a sheet of canvas over your head, and cooking on this pavement hard grains of rice boiled by the hot sun. These grains are so hard that they have to be chewed over and over again, in order to make believe that your stomach is really filled.

Now the most neglected and hungry people were surely the newborn babies. They could be found almost any morning on a rubbish-heap, on the steps of a police station or in a garbage can. One day the hand of God directed Mother Teresa to a large, unoccupied building near the Sisters' residence. She turned this yellow stucco building into an orphanage, calling it SHISHU BHAVAN, The Children's Home.

The first guest was a premature baby wrapped in a sheet of newspaper who had been picked off the street. He weighed less than three pounds and had not even the strength to suck from the bottle Mother Teresa gave him. But she persevered, and the baby became her first victory in this new haven of love.

Soon several dozens of babies were bundled together in cots and playpens. The Sisters and Father van Exem, their chaplain, were worried. How were they going to provide for so many people? After all, there were now several hundred mouths to be fed. But Mother Teresa was undismayed. She asked her helpers to draw up posters announcing that she would take in every child that was sent to her. "Money," she would say, "I never think of it. It always comes. The Lord sends it. We do His work; He provides the means. If He doesn't give us the means, that shows He does not want the work. So why worry?"

That shows how strong Mother Teresa's faith is. Now you should remember that this faith of hers doesn't just mean reciting "I believe in God the Father Almighty" and what not, the way we sometimes recite it quite mindlessly, or at least absentmindedly, on Sundays. It means that God is present to her here and now and always, walking with her at every moment, sheltering her with His loving providence.

# VIII

Although Mother Teresa does not worry about money, her practical sense tells her that she cannot accomplish her work without it. One day the chairman of a large company approached her to offer the missionaries a property in Bombay. He asked how her work was financed and what her budget was. She replied: "What made you come to me with your offer?" "I felt an urge inside me," he answered. "Well," she remarked, "other people like you come to see me, and they say the same. That is my budget."

Like one of her great patron saints, St. Teresa of Avila, she knows how to run things efficiently. When Pope Paul VI presented her with a luxurious white car, which had been provided by the Indian

Government for his visit, she arranged to raffle it off. That way she earned many times more than she would have by an outright sale.

She also set aside funds for the dowries of orphan girls who had grown up within her missions. A dowry is a property—sometimes only a kind of hope-chest with a certain number of saris—that a woman brings to her husband in marriage. Some people don't like this idea much. They quite rightly believe that this isn't a fair arrangement. But until the system is changed it is far better for a girl to have a dowry than not, for in India she will have a hard time finding a husband without one.

As Mother Teresa's projects expanded, it became necessary to travel quite a lot. What she didn't like was spending funds on airline tickets that could be spent on the poor. "Look," she pointed out to the attendant, "I am small enough to fit into the luggage rack"—and she was prepared to prove her point.

Another time she offered to work her way on Indian Airlines by serving as a stewardess. She insisted that her offer was serious, but the Indian Government turned it down. Since then she has been granted a free pass on all airlines and railways, a mark of respect usually reserved for the most important politicians.

# IX

Mother Teresa continued to rush to the aid of all those in desperate need. "I believe in person to person," she said, adding that, to her, every person was Christ. The poor, she said, deserve not only service and dedication, but also the joy that comes from human love. That is the thing we all have to grow in—that baffling, simple thing called love. It is, as you probably have realized by now, the great secret, the primary energy. It is the primary power by which we help others, whereby we help heal them, and help lift them up. It is the power that enabled Mother Teresa to now turn to the most wretched and neglected of people, the lepers. Leprosy is a dreadfully crippling and disfiguring disease, so much so that during the Middle Ages lepers were obliged to wear a bell around their necks, to warn people of their approach. To this day those who suffer from the disease are thrown out of society. Their relations, even their children, don't wish to see them anymore. Imagine if someone you love suddenly said: "I don't care about you any longer." If someone you love were to say this to you, would you not die a bit? Now these people, who are often well-educated and who hold high positions, travel far away from home, so that nobody can recognize them, and they are forced to go begging.

Mother Teresa constructed a special building outside the city for the worst cases, providing medicines and care, enveloping them with love. She often said that the worst disease any human being could ever experience was being unwanted. "Love each of them," she told her helpers; "love each of them with all your might."

But that was only the beginning. Next she dispatched groups of Indian Sisters out into the city, to open seven more dispensaries. But an employee at the town hall protested against such unpleasant neighbors and threatened to alert the authorities. Eventually Mother Teresa was forced to give in. But as so often before, she knew how to turn a defeat into victory. "What we need," she told her sisters, "are mobile clinics." And soon small white vans,

bearing the emblem of the Missionaries of Charity, were patrolling the enormous city to bring treatment into the most neglected areas.

# X

At this point you may well wonder what it is that enables Mother Teresa to love each person in such a particular and extraordinary way. How can she spend herself so utterly, so unceasingly, without exhausting her resources? Perhaps you have listened to a text of St. Paul on Sunday, in which he says: "I have made a libation of myself." And if you look up "libation" in the dictionary you will find "the pouring of a liquid, usually wine, in honor of a deity." Now Mother Teresa is a person who continually pours herself out. How is it, then, that she is never spent? If your mother writes out a lot of checks, fresh funds have to flow into her account at some point; otherwise there will be a notice

in the mail saying: "OVERDRAWN! Your account has been overdrawn because of insufficient funds."

Why, do you think, are Mother Teresa's "funds" never exhausted and who is it that replenishes them? The fullness within her is not exhausted because it does not derive from a human source. The mysterious source is the Holy Spirit Himself, Who dwells in her, and He is, of course, inexhaustible. The man or woman who possesses that Spirit fully can keep pouring and pouring and pouring, and there can be no question of ever running out.

Every morning at 6:30, Mother Teresa attends Mass at the small, second-floor chapel of the motherhouse on Lower Circular Road in Calcutta. At dawn, every day she prays there with her Sisters and novices. In the Holy Eucharist she receives the spiritual food which nourishes her, and without which, she has often said, she could not get through one single day of the life she has chosen.

After Mass the sisters wash their single change of clothes in shiny tin buckets, and then—armed with loaves of bread provided by English schoolchildren—they take off in all directions: some to schools and clinics, some to the lepers, and some to the Children's Home. Whatever they do, they do vigorously and with abounding joy.

What accounts for Mother Teresa's success? How could this slight foreign-born woman succeed so remarkably, beginning her work in a Communist-ruled city in a Hindu country? How had she, with a mere five rupees and no powerful backers, been able to assemble her worldwide empire of love? If you look at it in your atlas, it is amazing how far this empire of hers is stretching: centers have been established across the continents, in the Bronx, in Yemen, in Jordan, in London, in Venezuela, in Rome, and in several African countries. And while you are reading this, they are still growing.

Mother Teresa is one of those rare people who can directly translate her pure passions into action. She is what we would all like to be, if we weren't so double-minded and dispersed all over the lot: a person through whom the light of God shines.

# XI

Even before it was announced that Mother Teresa was to receive the Nobel Prize for Peace—the highest such honor in the world—part of her days were spent in DARSHAN, an Indian custom, in which the powerful, the famous, and the holy make themselves available to all seekers.

Some of those who came to see her did so as supplicants. Others brought gifts and touched her feet in homage. Among those waiting one morning was a young crippled man who said: "I am here because Mother loves me." Now do you believe that he came all this way, standing in line for hours, no doubt, because Mother Teresa has a universal love for the human race? I suspect not. He came because for her, at that moment, he was the only person in the world and he felt comforted and reassured. That is what the crippled man had meant when he explained his presence at the *darshan*.

There were also some well-dressed businessmen in the crowd who sought her autograph, asking her to write her name on perhaps ten sheets of paper. You would expect her to say: "Thank you very much, but I have better things to do. How dare you exploit me?" In all likelihood, that was what they had in mind, seeking to exploit her celebrity, planning to sell her autographs for a lot of money. She may have well realized that, but it didn't matter. They asked her to do something that was in her power, and, because it is her nature to give, she did it.

The evening before Mother Teresa received the Nobel Prize, Calcutta's largest newspaper proclaimed the glad tidings: THE MOTHER OF BENGAL IS NOW THE MOTHER OF THE WORLD! Her first response was "I am unworthy." There were, she said, so many people in the world wiser than she, better educated. "But I know the prize is not for me, that it is for the poor, and that I am receiving it on their behalf, isn't that so?" It is clear that she thought that the honor as well as the money was meant for the poor.

That day in Oslo, in front of the television cameras and the notables from all over the world, stood a small, slight woman in a white sari. The large lec-

tern seemed almost to swallow her up. If all the important people had come to Norway expecting a long and formal acceptance speech, they were disappointed. What Mother Teresa told them was to love each other, as God loved each of them.

On her return to Calcutta the Marxist government of West Bengal honored her with an official reception, something Marxist governments don't often do for a Roman Catholic nun. The federal government of India gave an equally official party in New Delhi, which is the capital of India. For days the motherhouse on Lower Circular Road was mobbed by friends, tourists, photographers, and fans. With grace Mother Teresa made herself available to all. Finally, it became too much. She felt that all that adulation was somewhat harmful.

She announced that she would observe a month of silence.

# XII

When we read about the lives of holy men and women, we come to understand that their achievements and victories are of the inward sort: they lived secluded lives, and God and the angels alone know of their triumphs.

Well, Mother Teresa was to experience a moment of triumph that the entire world was able to watch. Not that there wasn't suffering as well: we know, don't we, that the greatest sorrow and the greatest joy existed together at Golgotha, where Christ gave up His life for us. Anyhow, Mother Teresa wouldn't have expected it to happen any other way.

On February 3, 1986, Pope John Paul II came to visit her in the HOME FOR THE PURE IN HEART, in the midst of the Calcutta slums. More than 100,000 peo-

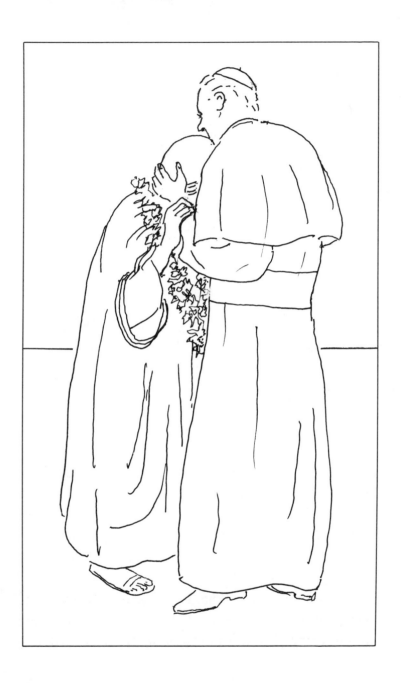

ple—boys and girls in school uniforms, people in traditional dress, and those who wore just rags—lined the streets as the Pope's motorcade entered town. The streets around Mother Teresa's house were jammed with Hindus and Moslems and Catholics—mostly Hindus, really, because Catholics in Calcutta are few and far between.

Why had they come? To get a glimpse of the Pope. "Just the glimpse of a religious person does good," said a Hindu policeman. And the Pope was certainly a religious person, he added. Another Hindu onlooker said that the crowds were there because of Mother Teresa: "Mother Teresa is a holy mother to all Calcutta, and not only that, to all India," he said. "And she is the only young lady who sacrifices her own entertainment and dedicates herself to the downtrodden people of Calcutta." Now it's funny, isn't it, that he called her a "young lady," Mother Teresa who won the Nobel Prize and is seventy-five years old. What he probably wanted to express, somehow, was that in spite of all that, she was delightful and young, and worthy of all the admiration and homage a man could render her.

At the Pope's arrival the crowds burst into cheers. Mother Teresa, a slight figure in her white and blue habit, knelt before him to kiss his ring, but he quickly drew her up, kissing her on the head and embracing her warmly.

They climbed a great platform together and she

placed a garland of flowers around his neck. To the applause of the crowd, the Pope took the garland off and placed it on Mother Teresa instead. If you have heard of "great moments in history," this was surely one of them—a whole lifetime wrapped up and summarized and rewarded. I'll bet you can't remember a woman ever honored in quite as splendid a fashion.

The Pope then visited the patients, making the rounds. He carried trays of food and served about a dozen of them. One old man he fed by spoon. A woman cried out in Bengali, and the Pope asked Mother Teresa to translate. "She's saying she's very, very alone, and she's telling you, 'Come back!' " The Pope took the woman's head in his hands and gently kissed her forehead. He was at a loss for words.

There isn't very much that one can say at such a moment, is there? Do you think if you had been there you would have known what to say? Hardly. You may be able to say "There, there." Such moments as deep as these are not to be met with words but only with silence.

The Pope could have easily said that we all have to suffer, that it is the result of Adam's sin—which is ours also—and that Christ, too, had suffered. This is all perfectly true, and good sound doctrine, but it isn't what a person in great anguish is ready to hear.

To the people gathered outside he said: "I cannot fully answer all your questions. I cannot take away all your pains. But of this I am sure: God loves you with an everlasting love. You are precious in His sight. In Him, I love you too. For in God, we are truly brothers and sisters."

Then Mother Teresa and the Pope rode in the Popemobile together, to the cheers of thousands of grateful people. Mother Teresa said: "This is the happiest day of my life."

*"As long as you did it to one of these My least brethren,
You did it to Me."*